Catch an Angel's Wing

Catch an Angel's Wing

A Christian View of Death

by
Gene Van Note

Beacon Hill Press of Kansas City
Kansas City, Missouri

All scripture quotations unless otherwise designated are from the
King James Version. Permission to quote from the following copy-
righted versions is acknowledged with appreciation:

New English Bible (NEB), © The Delegates of the Oxford University Press and The Syndics of the Cambridge University Press,
1961, 1970.

New International Version of the New Testament (NIV), © 1973
by the New York Bible Society International.

The *New Testament in Modern English* (Phillips), Revised Edition,
© J. B. Phillips, 1958, 1960, 1972. By permission of The Mac-
millan Publishing Co., Inc.

The Living Bible (TLB), © 1971 by Tyndale House Publishers,
Wheaton, Ill.

New American Standard Bible (NASB), © The Lockman Foundation, 1960, 1962, 1968, 1971, 1972, 1973, 1975.

Modern Language Bible, New Berkeley Version in Modern English,
(NBV), copyright © 1945, 1959, 1969 by Zondervan Publishing House.

Dedication

To
Lillie R. Goodwin
She is experiencing the joy we
anticipate.

Contents

1/

Single File

The young pastor quietly closed the door behind him. He was relieved to see that the hall was empty. No conversation necessary, no explanations required, he sat down on a nearby couch. Its solid support was welcome. It felt good to relax. He had just been through the most exhausting 60 minutes of his life.

"Mother is dying! Come quickly!" Those terrifying words, shouted in panic over the phone, had signaled the start of this unusual episode. Moments later he was in his car headed for the hospital 10 miles across a busy city.

The afternoon traffic was sparse. He had time to think, time to prepare himself for his first experience with a family in grief. An elder member of his congregation had been admitted to the hospital several days earlier. After a difficult 24 hours there were indications that she was making some improvement. The family was cautiously optimistic. They allowed themselves to begin to believe that their 80-year-old mother would recover from the massive stroke she had suffered.

Then the phone rang!

He wondered how he would react in the presence of death. It was an important question that would soon be answered. He paused outside the door for a moment. Then, breathing deeply, he walked into the darkened hospital room, trying to exhibit a confidence he did not feel.

Strangely, it was just as he expected. The two daughters seemed riveted to the wall, the fear in their eyes expressed in the convulsive sobs that shattered the silence. Their attention was focused on the nurse who was working frantically on the frail form of their loved one.

"She is so agitated, we thought you could help," the older daughter volunteered an answer to an unasked question.

"I don't understand it," the nurse muttered to herself, "that shot was big enough to put a horse to sleep."

"What did you say?" the pastor asked.

"I said, 'Perhaps I'd better call a doctor,'" she replied, lying to protect her professional status, and her job.

"Let me talk with her," the pastor suggested.

"She'll never hear you," the nurse whispered to him alone, "she is so upset she'll never know what you say. But go ahead, it won't hurt anything."

Apparently in a coma, the patient had been given an injection to relieve the intense pain. Obviously the narcotic had not helped. She writhed in agony.

Now everything was focused on him. The inexperienced clergyman moved to the side of the bed, his mind racing. What could he do? Suddenly he recalled the words of a seminary professor in a class he had taken not long before, "Always call a patient by name, even if they are unconscious. Sometimes they can hear but cannot speak."

Taking her hand he said, "Mrs. Hershey, this is your pastor. If you can hear me, squeeze my hand." Promptly the question was answered with an almost imperceptible but very real tightening of her hand muscles.

He knew what to read. The woman who now struggled against the pain had been a semi-invalid for months. Each week he visited her, reading from the "big print" Bible which rested on her nightstand.

Placing his own Bible on a nearby table, while holding her hand, he read,

"The Lord is my shepherd; I shall not want. . . . he leadeth me . . . The Lord is the strength of my life; of whom shall I be afraid? . . . They that wait upon the Lord shall renew their strength . . . they shall . . . not faint" (Ps. 23:1, 3; 27:1; Isa. 40:31).

Then, turning to the New Testament, he continued, "Let not your heart be troubled . . . I go to prepare a place for you. . . . In my father's house are many mansions . . . Peace I leave with you, my peace I give unto you . . . Let not your heart be troubled, neither let it be afraid" (John 14:1-2, 27).

He paused. During the 10 minutes he had been reading from the Bible some major changes had taken place. It was quiet now in the hospital room. The hysterical sobbing had ceased. A big tear splashed on the open Bible. For the first time he was aware that he was crying. A quick glance revealed that everyone in the room also was crying, including the tough special nurse who claimed to be an atheist.

Even the little lady was calm. He felt a slight touch on his hand. Clearing his husky throat, he went on with the reading of God's Word, "I saw a new heaven and a new earth . . . and God shall wipe away all tears from their eyes; and there shall be no more death, neither sorrow, nor crying, neither shall there be any more pain: for the former things are passed away. . . . the Spirit and the bride say, Come. And let him that heareth say, Come. And let him that is athirst come. And whosoever will, let him take the water of life freely. . . . Amen. Even so, come, Lord Jesus" (Rev. 21:1, 4; 22:17; 22:20).

Her hand relaxed completely. The pastor laid it gently by the side of this beautiful Christian who had walked with the Lord for nearly three-quarters of a century.

He stepped back. The room was filled with peace. Everyone stood quietly, as if in a cathedral. Then the young pastor turned to the door. Quietly he closed it behind him as he stepped into the deserted hall, not knowing that the woman to whom he had just ministered would never have another conscious moment.

The nearby couch was welcome. It provided full support, mental and physical. Later he would try to understand the meaning of it all. But, for now, it was enough to let the mind slip into neutral and the body sag against the cushions.

Abruptly the door opened. He resented the intrusion. It was the rough-speaking, cynical nurse. She, too, was struggling with her emotions, brushing away the tears with the back of her calloused hand. The experience in the hospital room had touched a long-hidden secret spring of faith and devotion.

They sat silently for some time. Finally, her emotions under reasonable control, she confessed, "That was the most beautiful worship service I've ever been in. Thank you."

Before he could respond, the quietness of the hospital hall was pierced by the wail of an infant baby.

"What's that?" asked the surprised pastor, alerted by the unexpected sound.

"It's a little baby," the nurse replied, "the newborn baby nursery is right there," pointing to a room barely 15 feet away.

With that she made her exit to recover her composure and rebuild her coarse exterior.

Alone once again a new thought flashed into the pastor's mind. Less than a dozen feet from each other, separated only by a thin wall, was the beginning and the ending of life. On his right happy parents were joyfully saying "Hello!" to their new baby; while on the left, brokenhearted children were saying "Good-bye" to their aged mother. As the apostle Paul wrote, the "new life . . . passed on to you from your parents . . . will fade away. . . . our natural lives will fade as grass does when it becomes all brown and dry" (1 Pet. 1:23-24, TLB). In life we may have moments of great joy and build relationships that provide relaxation and the opportunity for spiritual growth. But at the end of life, as it was in the beginning, we are alone.

In death, as in birth, we walk single file. The meaning of that narrow door with the "exit" sign above and the unknown beyond, is the subject of our search. The Holy Word and the best of human experience will help us prepare for that inevitable walk we all shall take,

Single file!

2/

Through an Open Door

"Death is a black camel that kneels once at every man's door," says an ancient Turkish proverb. Sooner or later that door is opened for every man. When it happens, he has no choice. He must climb on the black camel for a one-way trip into the trackless desert.

The Bible echoes the human experience, "Man is destined to die" (Heb. 9:27, NIV).

For all that is divine in man, he is still distressingly human. That is his agony. There is a lack of permanence in everything. His skin is smooth at 7 and wrinkled at 70. But even at 7, he is marked for death. In fact, the moment a child is born he is old enough to die. As the apostle Paul notes, "This precious treasure . . . is held in a perishable container, that is, in our weak bodies" (2 Cor. 4:7, TLB).

The transciency of life prompted Henry Ward Beecher to reflect, "We are not as necessary as we think. The sun will come up tomorrow if you do die. The stars will shine if you are not here to see them. Summer will come if your plow is still. The world is not made to turn on you as a pivot. You occupy a very small place."[1]

No wonder the human race has been referred to as "blood clots on a clod!" Some have concluded that if life has so little value, then death is the final disaster.

Aristotle said, "Death is a fearful thing, for it is the end." The ancient Greek, Aeschylus, agreed, "When earth once drinks the blood of a man, there is death once and for all and there is no resurrection." The best they could say was, "Farewell!" Farewell without hope; the final sad good-bye of an empty dream. Thus the poet Swinburne wrote,

> *From too much love of living*
> *From hope and fear set free*
> *We thank with brief thanksgiving*
> *Whatever gods may be*
> *That no life lives forever;*
> *That dead men rise up never*
> *That even the weariest river*
> *Winds somewhere safe to sea.*[2]

Bertrand Russell, too, was convinced that death is a dreary descent into nothing, as he makes clear in these words, "No fire, no heroism, no intensity of thought can preserve one individual life beyond the grave." Death for such persons becomes the "all-enveloping, all-consuming finality," as Paul Rees has observed.

Whatever it means, the black camel kneels at every-man's door.

In the devastating emotional upheaval that followed his wife's death, C. S. Lewis wrote in despair, "We were setting out on different roads. This cold truth. This terrible

15

traffic regulation (You, Madam, to the right—you, Sir, to the left)."[3]

Death is real!

The Mary Tyler Moore television program built its comedy, in one program, on an improbable foundation—the death of Chuckles, the clown. Murray, the newswriter, commented that it was not proper to take the death of a friend so lightly. Lou Grant, producer of the program's fictional news show replied, "We laugh at death because death will have the last laugh on us."

Tragically death does more than laugh.

In life's carefree hours, death can be accepted as a fact, even treated as a joke. But when it arrives, it often has a ghastly color. Except on occasions which are far too rare, death is a hostile, loathsome reality that turns the spirit numb and fills the heart with fear.

Primitive man reacted in an irrational manner. He built a buffer around his grief to insulate himself from the intensity of his loss. His strange rituals have no meaning to this sophisticated generation. Modern man is convinced that the gods cannot be appeased by the burning of monkey bones, nor can the dead be helped by placing rice and a blowgun on their graves.

Yet, with all his technological advancement, the 20th-century pagan still has not pushed back the dark borders of the unknown far enough to drain it of its terror. When the black camel comes to kneel at the door of a loved one, he reacts as irrationally as any person ever has.

Karl was 32 years of age, but he walked up the hill like he was 90. Stumbling on an unseen snag he would have fallen had it not been for the clergyman who walked with him.

They paused. The hill was not steep but it took him away from the open grave waiting to receive his father. His

16

grief made the hill too difficult to climb, at least for the moment.

Everyone was gone. The cars were unwinding themselves from the arena of sorrow. It was a quiet, beautiful spring day; the kind that fills a person with the exuberance of life.

But Karl had death on his mind. "I can't leave him, I can't. Oh, it's so hard, it's so hard."

Turning to the minister who had just officiated at his father's funeral he asked, "Do you know why it's so hard?"

Without waiting, he answered his own question, "It's so hard because it's so final."

Karl had no faith in the future, thus he had no hope in the present. A modern pagan, he was engulfed in a black, smothering finality.

This modern wail is an expression of an old malady. A papyrus from the second century B.C. claims, "Truly there is nothing anyone can do in the face of death." Many would readily agree, but not everyone. Some people have been able to do as William Cullen Bryant advised. They have lived so that when their time came they could be like "one who wraps the drapery of his couch about him and lies down to pleasant dreams."

A young lady, through her suffering, had gained a maturity not normal for one who had lived only 20 years. She had lost the battle with bone cancer but had won in the realm of the spirit. With assurance she said, "Dying is beautiful. People don't realize that death is a part of life. But you come to accept this, and I learned a lot about myself in the process."[4]

Many Christians, having seen beyond the "exit" sign, say "good-bye" without a trace of fear. They eagerly anticipate their next great adventure with the God of love and peace. Through their faith, even though they know they are dying, they have reached a new level of serenity. They can look the black camel in the eye and smile.

Sister Mary dePaul is the assistant to the chaplain at St. John's Hospital in Oxnard, Calif. Out of her experience she recounts that, for Christians, dying can be a peaceful event. "For some people," she says, "the prospect of death is so beautiful that when you hear them talk about it you say to yourself, 'That sounds so beautiful, can I come too?'"

The apostle Paul understood the dimensions of such a faith when he wrote that believers "sorrow not, even as others which have no hope" (1 Thess. 4:13).

Faith that can face the end without fear does not deny the existence of death. Death, frightful for the pagan, is just as real for the Christian. In their humanity they, too, experience the terrifying agony of life's final separation. The strength of our faith is that Christ can give victory over death and comfort in it.

Yet, death hurts. Deeply.

It was not a denial of his faith for a devout Christian to say at the close of a testimonial dinner, "Gentlemen, I appreciate what you have done for me tonight. But it doesn't mean much to me now. My wife died last year and I have no one to tell it to."

The poem "After the Burial" was written by James Russell Lowel from the reservoir of his own sorrow. The major portion of the piece was composed after the death of his daughter, Rose. Before the poem was completed his little son and his wife had also died. Following this soul-shattering experience he penned these final four lines,

> That little shoe in the corner,
>   So worn and wrinkled and brown,
> With all its emptiness confutes you
>   And argues your wisdom down.[5]

The Christian faith does not deny the inevitability of

life's encounter with the dark unknown. Everyone must pass through the valley of the shadow from which no one returns and around which there is no detour. No believer need apologize for the numbness that paralyzes the spirit. When Christians grieve it is not a denial of their faith but an affirmation of their capacity to love and be loved.

The widely-read Christian writer C. S. Lewis expressed this eloquently in *A Grief Observed*, where he records the intensely personal account of his reaction to the death of his wife, Joy Davidman. Early in this memoir of sorrow he groaned, "The sharp, cleansing tang of her otherness is gone. What pitiable cant to say, 'She will live forever in my memory!' *Live*—that is exactly what she won't do."[6]

But faith triumphs. Personal peace replaces fear and anger. Toward the end of his reflections on grief he remembers, "How wicked it would be, if we could, to call the dead back! She said, not to me but the chaplain, 'I am at peace with God.' She smiled, but not at me.'[7]

The Christian is not exempt from life's ultimate sorrow, but that is not the end of the tale. There is more beyond and it is better. In fact, that is exactly what Paul wrote to the Philippians, "For me, living means opportunities for Christ, and dying—well, that's better yet!" (Phil. 1:21, TLB).

Writing from a prison cell, Paul was eye-to-eye with the black camel, but he did not blink. He had a faith that transcended death. Years earlier, in an encounter with Jesus Christ on the road to Damascus, he had died to himself and his own selfish plans for his life. His destiny was in the hands of his loving Lord. Death was not going to be the end for him. It was in the jail at Philippi that Paul, and his friend Silas, had sung hymns of praise to God. Had it been written then, Paul would certainly have sung the beautiful Negro spiritual,

> Goin' home, goin' home, I'm just goin' home;
> It's not far, just close by—through an open door.

"Now we know," the apostle wrote to his friends, "that if the earthly tent we live in is destroyed, we have a building from God, an eternal house in heaven, not built by human hands (2 Cor. 5:1, NIV). That house will last forever.

At the time of bereavement, the sorrowing seek answers. They know that death has power and wonder, "Does life have meaning?" The Bible replies, "Of course it does," and provides the atmosphere of faith in which the answer can be found.

For some, those biblical answers come more readily because of their knowledge of the Word. The reservoir has been filled daily during their prayer time. The Bible is like a dear and trusted friend with whom they share every experience, both the happy and the sad. Its resources are meaningful because they reflect the personal relationship they have with its Author.

Thus an elderly woman remembered the day when the angish of the Second World War became intensely personal. Her brother was a prisoner of the Japanese, when a telegram arrived from the War Department informing her of the death of her only son. Stunned by this tragic news she thumbed through her well-worn Bible seeking comfort. She found it in the psalms as she read, "Blessed is the man that feareth the Lord . . . He shall not be afraid of evil tidings . . . [for] God is our refuge and strength, a very present help in trouble" (Ps. 112:1, 7; 46:1). Later she testified, "God became my strength when trouble came in a yellow telegram."

On other occasions, sorrow confirms the reality of a lifelong faith. A retired clergyman who had buried his wife of 52 years less than 24 hours earlier shared his inmost feelings with an old friend, "I have proven the grace of God. I have stood many times with people at a time like this, and I thought I understood what they were going through. But I did not know before how good God can be. This verse has been going through my mind again and again, 'Fear thou

20

not; for I am with thee; be not dismayed; for I am thy God: I will strengthen thee; yea, I will help thee; yea, I will uphold thee with the right hand of my righteousness'" (Isa. 41:10).

In their own way, each of these Christians had proven the grace of God to be adequate under the most devastating circumstances. What they did not realize in the early hours of their sorrow was that bereavement is not like a mathematical problem; once solved, life has a way of getting tangled again. When that happens, life can be rebuilt with the compassionate understanding of a kind friend.

A university professor teaches a class called simply "Love." It is so popular that students must put their name on a waiting list in order to enroll in the class. One unique feature of his class is the requirement that every student must spend a minimum of 30 hours during the semester doing something for someone else.

One day a young man named Joel came to him. Joel was from a very wealthy family. He had never been required to do anything in his life and, consequently, did not know where to start nor where to go to help anyone. The professor sent him just a few blocks down the street from the university to an "old folks' home." It was a dreary place where the old ladies stayed in ugly flannel nightgowns and the men never combed their hair or put on their dress clothes. They just lived in their pajamas.

Joel went in, and soon came tumbling out—horrified! He never knew anyone existed on that level. But he went back. Week after week he went back. First, it was for two hours a week. Then, four hours a week. He would simply sit by someone's bed and talk. Not about anything special, just about the world outside: school, life, ordinary things.

The residents of that home began to gather around Joel when he arrived. Soon his visits became known as "Joel's Days." The ladies, known for their drabness, began to ask their families to bring them some fancy bedclothes they could wear on "Joel's Days." The men began to shave and dress up on the day when they knew Joel would come.

What made the difference? Someone cared!

"In the name of compassion," says Janet Kern, "don't subject a bereaved person to high-sounding cliches such as 'Time heals.' He won't believe it; he will believe simply that you don't realize the depth of his sorrow. 'After a while you'll forget,' is equally painful. The last thing in the world one wants is to forget. Above all, refrain from indulging in that most arrogant of condolence cliches, 'He would have wanted you to . . .' Advice is not consolation."[8]

The eternal solace of the Word of God coupled with the ever-present warmth of a Christian friend are God's prescription for the deep personal agony of final seperation.

3/

It All Depends
on the Liver

She held a cold cup of coffee with the same gentleness that she held the memory of her boy. For more than an hour the words had tumbled out as she talked with her pastor.

Then, silence.

There were no tears either.

Two days of uncontrollable crying had drained the fountain of grief.

It had happened on a sunny Sunday afternoon. Her impulsive 11-year-old boy, ignoring the flashing red lights and clanging bell, had ridden his bicycle into the path of a train. In that moment, her happy boy had been killed in full view of his 8-year-old brother.

The tears had ceased to flow long before the torrent of words had stopped. Now it was time for reflection; time to consider all those unanswered questions.

Finally she broke the silence as she tried to put this irrational happening into reasonable form. Speaking more to herself than to anyone else she said quietly, "If only I knew that there would be other children in heaven because he lived, then I think I could stand it." Unconsciously, in her unrelieved sorrow, she had stumbled over one of the questions that mock men at the point of their greatest weakness.

Death has power, does life have meaning? This ancient question is tied to many a modern sorrow.

Does the Christian faith have anything to say to the charge that death is life out of control; that it's a cancer on the heartbeat of mankind? If it does, then it should say it clearly and often. If not, then it should quietly close its Holy Book and become a part of history; a good idea that did not work, the dusty relic of a sterile past.

The grieving mother's search for meaning is very common. Bereavement is an intensely personal experience. Life is reduced to one dimension, memory. Such a period of reflection is normal and can be very helpful, as it was in the life of a man who had just buried his wife after 52 years of married life together. He received many cards and letters which contained expressions of sympathy and messages of condolence. Of all of them, the one that helped him the most simply said, "You lucky guy. You got to spend a half-century with the best person God ever made. You must have a lot of happy memories." As he recalled the highlights of a happy life his gloom began to lift.

For most people, healing begins with the warmth and love of friends who really care. This was the testimony of an elderly lady who sent this note to her church, "You gave me encouragement when I was so down and it was hard to see the little beam of light at the end of a seemingly endless tunnel of darkness. I do not have the words to tell you what a blessing you have been to me."

This "conspiracy of love" is Christianity's first answer to the question, "Death has power, does life have meaning?"

The apostle Paul instructed the Christians in Corinth, "Now here is what I am trying to say: All of you together are the one body of Christ and each of you is a separate and necessary part of it. If one part suffers, all parts suffer with it, and if one part is honored, all the parts are glad" (1 Cor. 12:27, 26, TLB). Changing the picture, he advised the believers in Rome, "Be devoted to one another in brotherly love. Honor one another above yourselves. . . . Rejoice with those who rejoice; mourn with those who mourn" (Rom. 12:10, 15, NIV). The current interest in the "Body of Christ" with emphasis on members ministering to one another is Christian love in action. It is the most basic expression of the New Testament faith.

Sometimes, however, even those who love the most do not understand how sorrow depletes the normal reserves of energy. A young widow, trying to recover from the shock of her husband's sudden death confided to a visitor, "My friends at the church say, 'Be strong,' without realizing that it takes all my strength just to get out of bed and face the day alone." At that point she needed the comfort and presence of someone who had successfully worked their way through similar sorrow. The touch on the shoulder, a smile, a companion in tears, an hour's silent communion with the one who had been there and had come back, can provide more consolation than a thousand words from the uninitiated.

Anyone who has experienced the lonely despair of bereavement would not be critical of the woman whose strength was at such a low ebb. Yet even they might reflect that this is not how God intended people to live. The Psalmist sings of the glory of man,

25

When I consider Thy heavens,
  the work of Thy fingers,
The moon and the stars,
  which Thou hast ordained;
What is man, that Thou dost
  take thought of him? . . .
Yet Thou hast made him
  a little lower than God,
And dost crown him with glory
  and majesty!
Thou dost make him to rule
  over the works of
  Thy hands;
Thou hast put all things under
his feet (Ps. 8:3-6, NASB).

What a contrast! The most powerful creature on earth, endowed with the divine right of dominion lacking sufficient strength to get out of bed and face the day alone.

Is this deficiency restricted to just one widow? Hardly! It is the common malady of mankind. Man, as William Barclay notes, is "a creature frustrated by his temptations, girt about with his weakness. He who should be free is bound; he who should be a king is a slave."[1]

How did it happen?

Its origin is no mystery, as Paul notes in his letter to the Roman Christians: "Therefore, just as sin entered the world . . . and death through sin, and in this way death came to all men, because all sinned" (Rom. 5:12, NIV). All have sinned in Adam. Therefore all men are under the penalty of death. But that is not the end of the story. There is another chapter. "Since death came through a man, the resurrection of the dead comes also through a man. For as in Adam all die, so in Christ all will be made alive" (1 Cor. 15:21-22, NIV).

Our spiritual unity with Christ can be as real as our physical unity with Adam. First there is Adam: sin, death; then there is Christ: righteousness, life.

The writer to the Hebrews expresses this in a powerful statement of victory. Against the backdrop of future events he proclaims,

> We have not yet seen all of this take place, but we do see Jesus . . . crowned now by God with glory and honor because he suffered death for us. Since we, God's children, are human beings—made of flesh and blood—he became flesh and blood too by being born in human form; for only as a human being could he die and in dying break the power of the devil who had the power of death. Only in that way could he deliver those who through fear of death have been living all their lives as slaves to constant dread (Heb. 2:8-9, 14-15, TLB).

The exciting promise is that "in Christ shall all be made alive" (1 Corinthians 15:22). For, Christ announced, "I am he that liveth, and was dead; and, behold, I am alive for evermore, Amen; and have the keys of hell and of death" (Rev. 1:18).

What tremendous assurance! Jesus Christ voluntarily took on himself the limitations of humanity, including all its frustration, suffering, and death. He changed the nature of life's final event so drastically that Christians are able to say,

"O death, where is thy sting? O grave, where is thy victory? . . . thanks be to God, which giveth us the victory through our Lord Jesus Christ" (1 Cor. 15:55-56).

By His life, death, and glory, Christ has raised man back to the place God intended for him to live. A hospital X-ray technician noted the importance of Christ's sacrificial death when he told a pastor's conference, "Many times people give up before the body wears out. For Christ, His will to live and His will to die were the same. You can die for something. People who die for something are better off than those who die from something."

Christ died for something, to "free those who all their lives were held in slavery by their fear of death" (Heb. 2:15, NIV).

If this is true, then every human life is significant. Jesus would agree. "Are not two sparrows sold for a penny?" He asked. "Yet not one of them will fall to the ground apart from the will of your father. And even the very hairs of your head are all numbered" (Matt. 10:29-30, NIV).

The significance of one's life, however, is measured by more than its length. "Methusaleh lived 969 years and he died" (Gen. 5:27). This is one of seven references to him in the sacred record. In the other six he appears in a genealogical table, simply identified as a member of the human race. He illustrates the basic truth that there is more to life than length.

To have lived a long time is no guarantee that a person has added anything of beauty and dignity to the world. A cantankerous old gentleman was nearing the end of his stormy life. He had made many people unhappy and never went out of his way to bring a smile to anyone. He confided to an acquaintance, "I am going to die without an enemy in this world."

"You mean, you have been reconciled to everyone with whom you have argued and fought? Have they all forgiven you?"

"No," he crowed triumphantly, "but I've outlived every one of them!"

Contrast that with the fact that the person who made the greatest impact on history lived only 33 years. He lived in quiet isolation, in an obscure Roman province; an area that had the reputation for failure. "Can anything good come out of Nazareth?" His critics repeated a common question in their attempt to discredit Him.

His education was average; His parents were common folk. He was misunderstood by His family, rejected by His generation, and in the end, deserted by His closest friends. His life ended in the midst of horror and shame. He died as the enemy of the state, judged to be too dangerous to be allowed to live. Yet, Christian or not, no one anywhere in the world can escape His influence on their life. All this with only three years of public ministry.

Between Jesus and Methusaleh there is no contest. They illustrate the truth put into epigrammatic form, "Life is like a joke; what counts is not how long but how good it is."

Brevity is no guarantee of greatness either. An unknown author compared the Greek ruler Alexander the Great to Jesus Christ in these words,

> *Jesus and Alexander died at thirty-three.*
> *One lived and died for self,*
> *The other died for you and me.*

The value of life depends not on its extent but on its intent and content. It is not its duration but its divine quality that really matters.

In times of quiet reflection we seek for ways to instill life with dignity and purpose. At the time of sorrow and under the shadow of bereavement, this search becomes a mission. Those in grief long for a full measure of serenity in the soul to come home to at night and go out from in the morning.

Yet, as Harry Emerson Fosdick has noted, "No one can get inner peace by pouncing on it, by vigoriously willing to have it. Peace is a margin of power around our daily need."[2]

Peace is a dimension of power.

And so is happiness. Happiness is the result of an inner stability, not an outer security. It is not an accident. It does not drop out of the sky on "lucky" people. It is increasingly clear that this is not a haphazard world. On the contrary, it is a fundamentally dependable, entirely predictable world, where peaches grow on peach trees, not watermelon vines.

The human tendency is to externalize the search. The frantic pursuit of things to do, places to go, and stuff to swallow has a price tag amounting to billions of dollars each year.

But you cannot buy peace, or happiness. Happiness is the byproduct of wholeness, or to use the theological word, "holiness." As Dr. Hocking said, "Happiness is the state of going somewhere wholeheartedly and unanimously." From another perspective, "Here is the psychological soundness of the Christian teaching on conversion," says J. Wallace Hamilton, "when the total self is awakened, when the whole being comes alive unto God and begins to move somewhere unanimously, God puts the sound of laughter in the soul. The joy of conversion is the music of wholeness."[3]

These are comforting words, words of hope and joy; of gladness and victory. But, do they have any meaning to a mother sitting at her kitchen table with a full cup of cold coffee and an empty bedroom?

It would be absurd to think that words could revise history, or that even the kindest expression of love could mask the pain of personal loss. There is no easy way to mourn the dead, only the passage of time can bring healing to the broken spirit and the lonely soul.

However, there is confident assurance in the Holy Word that additional resources are available to the Christian. When Paul wrote, "So then encourage one another with these words" (1 Thess. 4:18), he was talking about something more meaningful than the passage of time. He spoke of the resources made available through Christ. God's promise is clear, "My grace is sufficient for you, for my power is made perfect in weakness" (2 Cor. 12:9, NIV). As W. T. Purkiser wrote, "We can never avoid trouble. It is part of life in a sin-cursed world. But whether we rise above trouble in victory or go down beneath it depends not on the hardships life brings to us, but on the way we react to them."[4]

Dr. Wilfred Grenfell, pioneer missionary to Greenland, spent a lifetime of treating a wide variety of health problems. Toward the end of his career he noted that often the thing that was troubling his patient was expressed in the question, "Doctor, is life worth living?"

To which he always replied, "That depends on the liver!"

The Christian, living in a dynamic relation with Jesus Christ, has learned that Christ has given life meaning. They know that even though death has power, Christ has given significance to life by becoming triumphant over death.

They have also learned a companion truth, "Life gives meaning to death."

4/

Life Gives Meaning to Death

The 24-inch world of color television makes it seem so simple. Two men meet at high noon on the dusty street of a long-forgotten frontier town. Instant recognition, followed by fear and rapid-fire shots from the ever-present six-shooter. A crowd appears instantly. Suddenly, a man bursts through the circle, falls on his knees, and placing his ear to the chest of the fallen gunfighter says, "It's too late to call the doc, he's gone!"

Hearing that cryptic announcement, the crowd fades away—to the saloon, the sheriff, and the undertaker.

It is not that routine in real life. To define death has become one of medical science's most difficult assignments. Primitive methods have been replaced by technical equipment. No longer is the doctor limited to feeling for a pulse or trying to observe the moisture of a faint breath on a mirror. He has at his disposal a wide variety of technical equipment. These sophisticated machines accurately and continuously measure everything from heartbeat to brain waves.

While some researchers have been developing this recording equipment, others have created some extremely useful lifesaving machines: blood is filtered, lungs expanded, the heart is assisted by a pump or prompted into action by the gentle jolt of an electric shock. Bodily functions can be maintained by this equipment, allowing healing to take place and life to continue. It is an incredible world.

But what if life cannot continue without external help? At what point does life cease and the body become simply a hollow form on a white sheet? When should the machines be turned off, and by whom? Unexpectedly, the development of these modern electronic devices has not helped the doctor make the most basic decision. In fact, it is more difficult to define death now than it ever has been in the history of the world.

The struggle to find a definition has moved from the quiet efficiency of the intensive care unit to the cold logic of the courtroom. The search is on for a medically sound, legally accurate definition of death. Again television carries the picture story. This time it is not an actor lying in the dust, but frustrated, grieving parents seeking in vain for the life-support equipment to be turned off. They are ready to accept the inevitable; a choice denied them by the confusion of our time.

Out of the controversy and sadness a definition will eventually emerge; a compromise between morality and expediency. For a few years it will be reasonably useful. Then additional developments will increase our ability to measure bodily functions or prolong life and the definition will have to be changed. No doubt, every generation from now to the end of the world will face the challenge of writing a new definition of death.

Yet every definition will have one thing in common: death will be defined in terms of life. Death cannot be defined apart from life. It has no character or quality of its own. It is this lack that necessitates a definition based upon what it is not. Death is the cessation—the ultimate, final, irremediable cessation of life.

If death is difficult to define, it is even more difficult to disregard. Death does not lose any of its reality through imprecise definition. It takes more than the manipulation of language to change reality.

In his penetrating novel *The Robe*, Lloyd C. Douglas has this conversation take place between Marcellus, the Roman soldier who was in charge of Christ's crucifixion, and his slave Demetrius. It begins with Demetrius quoting from the Roman philosopher, Lucretius.

"'Lucretius thinks it is the fear of death that makes men miserable,' went on Demetrius, 'he's for abolishing that fear.'

"'A good idea,' argued Marcellus languidly, 'How does he propose to do it?'

"'By assuming that there is no future life,' explained Demetrius.

"'That would do it,' drawled Marcellus—'provided the assumption would stay where you had put it.'"[1]

Our attitude toward life's final event does not change its inevitability. "Up to the very last link," writes Dr. Felix Marti-Ibanez, "life is a biochemical chain reaction. Once life is launched, like a bullet it must reach its final destination, which is death."[2] That is not to say, however, that death has the same meaning for everyone. It can bring sorrow or joy; be hated or loved; fought or welcomed. The carefully planned execution of a despised enemy prompts different emotions than the sudden accident that snuffs out the life of a child. Death draws its meaning from life, its meaning from what life means.

Men die like they live, simply because death is not a state but an act.

Hanging in a California home is a painting of a farm house and outbuildings which were a part of the landscape of western Kansas before the first World War. It has been lovingly sketched from an old wrinkled photograph and a bushel of happy memories. It was the childhood home of the artist. With obvious joy she will point out her upstairs bedroom and recount the pleasant memories of those earlier days.

The painting, the photograph rescued from the trash, and the memories are all that remain. Years ago, her brothers tore the old house down to make room for a much more comfortable modern home. But the wood was not destroyed. It was not used as kindling in the fireplace or raw material for a corral fence. They transported the wood from the "old home place" to the mountains near Pikes Peak, in Colorado. There they have built two cabins which they use for vacation and relaxation.

The old farmhouse is gone but the home remains. It continues, not only in memory, but also in a new form providing comfort and joy for the children of the last quarter of the century as it did for the children of the first quarter.

Biologists say that the human body goes through constant change. The old is constantly being replaced by the new, so that we have a new body every seven years. The old house is gone, and yet it remains.

Here is a radiant Christian, more than 80 years of age, known affectionately by family and friends as "Mrs. Mac." Her parents were part of the "Land-Rush" into Indian Territory, soon to become the state of Oklahoma. There she grew to be a young lady, reared her children, and buried her husband. Gone is the vigor of her youth, replaced by the tentative, uncertain movements of old age. She does not look like she did when she was 18, her hand is not as steady, nor her eyesight as clear. Yet there is an unmistakable spiritual identity that abides. The old house is gone, and yet it remains.

That is life: progress, change, and continuity. That is also death: the normal, natural part of a process. In fact, Jesus asserted that it was an absolutely essential part of the process of life. Speaking first of His own impending execution but quickly expanding it to every man, Jesus said, "Unless a grain of wheat falls into the earth and dies, it remains by itself alone; but if it dies, it bears much fruit. He who loves his life loses it; and he who hates his life in this world shall keep it to life eternal" (John 12:24-25, NASB).

One man remarked, "I'm not hurrying to leave this world. My reservations for the next have not been confirmed." Worldly-wise travelers of this sophisticated generation know how to confirm their reservations. An efficient ticket agent punches the code into a computer terminal. Moments later the answer is printed out on the quivering face of a TV tube. But how does one confirm his reservations to the desired destination in the next life? The great Christian leader of the first century, Paul, was confident he knew the answer. He confided to his friend Timothy that it is "by the appearing of our Saviour Jesus Christ, who hath abolished death, and hath brought life and immortality to light through the gospel" (2 Tim. 1:10).

This is in line with the words of Jesus, "For whoever wants to save his life will lose it, but whoever loses his life for me and for the gospel will save it" (Mark 8:35, NIV).

The comforting assurance of Jesus Christ is not a bit of nostalgia, the worn-out reminder of bygone days. The promises affirmed by Jesus and confirmed by Paul are still powerful and workable today. A successful businessman cancelled his busy schedule to fly home to his mother's bedside. Both knew it would be their final visit. At first they talked about life on the surface, "How was your trip? How is the family?" Soon it became evident that she wanted to talk about matters of greater significance.

"I may not be here at your next birthday," she said, quietly probing to see if her son had strength enough to face the doctor's grim diagnosis.

She was relieved when he replied, "Would you like to talk about it?"

Holding hands, as they had done when he was a child, they reminisced about the past and looked into the future, Finally, the strength and vitality of her great faith was evidenced when she said,

"The doctors tell me that I do not have long to live. People have wanted me to go to faith healers and do things like that. I'm not having as much trouble with the fact of my death as other people are. I can handle the big things in life because in the little things He has helped me every time."

This is a modern echo of an age-old testimony. The apostle Paul testified, "The time of my departure is at hand. I have fought a good fight, I have finished my course, I have kept the faith: Henceforth there is laid up for me a crown of righteousness, which the Lord, the righteous judge, shall give me at that day: and not to me only, but unto all them also that love his appearing" (2 Tim. 4:6-8).

This scriptural truth has found a modern ally in an unlikely place, psychological research. "The more complete one's life is, the more one's destiny and one's creative capacities are fulfilled, the less one fears death," says Lisl Marburg Goodman. Professor Goodman, of Jersey City (N. J.) State College, shared the results of a series of in-depth interviews with more than 600 people.

She told the American Psychological Association at

their annual meeting that "people are not afraid of death per se, but of the incompleteness of their lives."[2]

The more positive one feels about the past, the more complete life is in the present, the more one's destiny has been fulfilled, the less one fears death. That is the conclusion of psychological research. It parallels the Word of God, "We know that if the earthly tent we live in is destroyed, we have a building from God, an eternal house in heaven, not built by human hands. . . . Now it is God who has made us for this very purpose and has given us the Spirit as a deposit guaranteeing what is to come" (2 Cor. 5:1, 5, NIV).

William Barclay shares this incident. A man whose father was old and ill had gone up to his father's bedroom to begin the day. The father said, "Pull up the blinds so that I can see the morning light." As the son lifted the shades and the light entered the room the old man sank back on his pillow, dead. How wonderfully appropriate. In a very real way, death is like that for every Christian.

When life is lived on the high level of Christian joy, when life is at its best, we say, "This is worth keeping." Many a philosopher has argued, "Immortality ought to be true because the human personality is so valuable." Victor Hugo said about himself,

> For half a century I have been writing my thoughts in prose and verse; history, philosophy, drama, romance, tradition, satire, ode and song. I have tried it all. But I feel I have not said the thousandth part of what is in me. When I go down to the grave I can say like many others, 'I have finished my day's work,' But I cannot say, 'I have finished my life.' My day's work will begin again the next morning. The tomb is not a blind alley, but a thoroughfare. It closes on the twilight, opens on the dawn.

Faith in life hereafter can be our loftiest way of affirming the sanctity and significance of human life. The scripture declares that God has some exciting things in store for the believer: "No eye has seen, no ear has heard, no mind has conceived what God has prepared for those who love him" (1 Cor. 2:9, NIV).

Thus the greater challenge is not to prepare to die, but to become equipped to live. As a young boy wrote to Walter Russell Bowie when he was a soldier in France during the First World War, "I hope you live all your life."

A visitor to southern Oregon sat quietly on a flat rock at the edge of the scenic Rogue River. The sharp chill of the water on his bare feet was a welcome counterpart to the warm sun. Through the crystal clear water he noticed a small stone of rare beauty. It had delicate shades of purple and rose highlighting a unique river-formed shape. He picked it up, turned it over and over enjoying the changing color and design.

But as he held it the heat of the sun and the warmth from his hands dried the moisture from the small rock. As it dried it seemed to lose its vitality until it was dull, lifeless and uninteresting. Taken out of its natural element it had lost its beauty. Thus also the Christian. "For if a man is in Christ he becomes a new person altogether—the past is finished and gone, everything has become fresh and new" (2 Cor. 5:17, Phillips).

The issue, then, is life. Men die as they live. As Dr. Marti-Ibanez says, "Whatever incites us to die also incites us to live with greater intensity."[4]

Life gives meaning to death. The reverse is also true; death gives meaning to life.

5/

Death Gives Meaning to Life

Easter Sunday. The overflow crowd was leaving the church sanctuary following the worship service. Everyone was happy. The evangelism committee was thrilled because they had had to bring in folding chairs to seat the crowd. The finance committee was pleased with the size of the offering. The pastor was inspired by the sight of a packed auditorium.

Everyone was happy. That is, everyone but one.

The pastor had not preached a traditional sermon on the resurrection of Jesus that Easter morning. Instead of talking about Christ's new life he tried to get his listeners to consider the impact of Christ's life on their death. For at least one person the subject of death was taboo, an unwelcome intrusion into a traditionally lighthearted day. As that worshipper left the sanctuary she said,

"You have no right to force me to think about death. I came to the Easter service to hear about the Resurrection, not to be challenged about my dying. I want to know how to live, not how to die."[1]

Few people wish to talk about death, especially on a pleasant Sunday morning dressed in their bright, new clothes. Death is a subject reserved for antiseptic rooms, with the curtains drawn and voices barely above a whisper. "I want to know how to live, not how to die."

Most people would agree. The fear of death is shared by people from every culture and every economic level. No one lives many years until he or she experiences that numb, taut feeling in the throat that accompanies the terse announcement of final loss.

Yet, except in unusual cases, the act of dying may not be as painful as the living suppose. On the contrary, writes Dr. Felix Marti-Ibanez, editor and publisher of *MD* magaaine, "[Death] is suffused with serenity, even a certain well-being and spiritual exaltation, caused by the anesthetic action of carbon dioxide on the central nervous system."[2]

This physical phenomenon seems to be present even with many people who are suffering intense pain from accident or illness. An elderly lady, in the final stages of incurable heart disease, confided to her pastor 20 minutes before her death, "I don't know what is happening, but for the first time in weeks I don't feel any pain. I am at peace."

Often when the level of pain is more than the mind can bear, unconsciousness results. There is ample evidence to indicate that a person living on this subconscious level is not inert like a fallen log or a discarded stone. Some patients who have been through this have rallied to report that their near-death episode was peaceful and sometimes positively euphoric.

The case of an injured mill worker, while unusual, is not unique nor unknown to medical science. While adjust-

41

ing a gangsaw, he had fallen into the equipment, striking his head on a steel I beam. The pain, resulting from the skull fracture, was excruciating. For 10 days he was in a deep coma, more dead than alive. The doctors advised his wife that he would not live, and a compassionate union shop steward filled out the papers to speed up payment of death benefits to the shocked widow.

But he did not die. Unable to move a muscle, he was fully aware of what was happening in the hospital room. His hearing was extremely acute. He could tell the position of everyone in the room, the doctor and the special nurse who were frantically administering lifesaving equipment, his wife and the pastor who stood over against the wall.

Suddenly he heard the doctor say, "We've lost him, he's gone!"

Later, he said, that at that moment he seemed to be separated from his body, hovering above the classic scene of tragedy in the hospital room. As an observer rather than a participant, he saw the skillful, but unsuccessful efforts of the doctor, and his wife with her head on her pastor's shoulders, tears streaming down her face. He was at peace, experiencing the most sublime feeling of joy and gladness he had ever known. After a few moments, it seemed a voice said, "It's not time for you to die yet, you must return to your family." He argued with the voice, insisting that he did not want to return to the world of pain from this place of rest. Finally he agreed, seemed to reenter the lifeless form that lay on the hospital bed, and moments later opened his eyes and said, "Good morning, how is everyone?"

It was months later before he felt confident enough to share this intimate experience. Even then, he did not try to analyze it. Whether it was an actual experience or only the unfettered activity of his fevered mind, he did not know. He had neither the background nor the inclination to question it. For him, it was real and life-changing, His encounter with death gave him a new appreciation for life, investing each person with a new dignity and each day with glory.

About seven in the morning, on the day of his death, Dwight L. Moody said, "Earth is receding; heaven is opening; it is beautiful. If this is death, it is sweet; there is no valley here. God is calling and I must go." He slipped into a coma from which he returned only after considerable medication. Abruptly raising himself on one elbow he asked, "What does all this mean? What are you doing here? This is a strange thing. I have been beyond the gates of death to the very portals of Heaven, and here I am back again."[3]

Though this kind of seemingly psychic happening is probably more common than most people suppose, few people will voluntarily consider the fact of their own death. A congregation in the Midwest was asked to provide personal data for the pastor's file. He wanted to know how they would like their memorial service to be conducted. They were thrown into a turmoil.[4] Apparently, most of them never applied their beliefs to the ultimate issues of life and death. For that body of believers, Christ was a storybook figure of a bygone era, not a present-day personal Friend who had conquered death, and could help them do the same. They had never actually accepted the reality of Christ's promise, "Because I live, ye shall live also" (John 14:19). Thus they were unable to apply the resources of the Christian gospel to the challenge of living and preparation for dying.

What is clear is that the sense of the supernatural is often keener at the time of the death of a loved one, or at the moment of our own brush with infinity. As God distinctly called Abram on the occasion of the death of his father, Terah, God sometimes has His best chance to speak to us when our hearts are softened by loneliness.

Bishop Hans Lilje, while president of the Lutheran World Federation wrote *The Valley of the Shadow*. This account of his years in a Nazi concentration camp is an amazing testimony of faith under fire. He says, "To be brought face-to-face with death gives a certain nobility to a human being. Once fully to venture your life for a cause dear to you, cowardice and fear are banished. So I was able to go through these nightly scenes of hell, which increased more toward the end of the time, without any loss of confidence."[5]

No one can choose the circumstances of his birth and only the suicidal can arrange the conditions of his death, yet everyone can select the principles by which he will live. And every person must find his own reason for living.

The apostle Paul found that reason in Jesus Christ, "According to my earnest expectation and my hope, that in nothing I shall be ashamed, but that with all boldness, as always, so now also Christ shall be magnified in my body, whether it be by life, or by death. For to me to live is Christ, and to die is gain" (Phil. 1:20-21).

"If ye then be risen with Christ, seek those things which are above, where Christ sitteth on the right hand of God. Set your affection on things above, not on things on the earth. For ye are dead, and your life is hid with Christ in God" (Col. 3:1-3).

Thus a man could say of a close personal friend who had lived his life by the confident promises of the Risen Christ and had just crossed into that Better Land, "If scars are stars, then his pathway will be well lighted." Yet the redemptive light that shines from life's tragic happenings has little to do with the length of years. Rather, it flows from the triumphant faith of a trusting child of God.

Randy was just a month past his 14th birthday when his mother took him to the family doctor for a routine physical checkup. Athletic, healthy, happy—those were the words that described this robust young man, except that recently he had been tiring more quickly than the other teens. No longer could he play the entire game, and the previous week he had to be seated before the choir practice was completed.

"Growing pains." His father laughed. "You just need some vitamins and another hamburger."

Neither did the doctor seem troubled when he suggested the need for further tests. Yet there was something about the seriousness of his attitude that drove them to have the blood tests made immediately.

A few days' wait. A phone call.

"Could you come in right away, please," was all the doctor said. Minutes later Randy's parents sat in the medical office and heard the dreadful news, "We'll have to make further tests to confirm it, but our preliminary results show that Randy is suffering from an acute form of leukemia."

Leukemia! Blood cancer!

Suddenly their world crumbled. The next few months became a blur; an exhausting round of doctors' offices, laboratories, blood tests, and hospital rooms. The good days when everyone was optimistic were often followed, abruptly, by a new onslaught of the disease.

The doctor released Randy from the hospital one Friday in March so he could attend the choir retreat in the mountains. It was an invigorating spring morning as father and son enjoyed each other's company and the annual spectacle of nature coming alive.

"Let's stop here," Randy said quietly. Subdued, but relaxed, they walked through the pioneer cemetary at Shingletown. Later the young man said to his mother, "If anything happens that is where I'd like to be."

But that was eight months away. First there was the retreat where Randy's happy Christian faith lifted everyone. At least one choir member decided to become a Christian that day because of the joy and vigor of a young teenage boy who was condemned to die but was not imprisoned by anger nor immobilized by fear.

Yet the rugged killer marched on relentlessly. Randy's deterioration could be seen in the tired lines in his mother's face; lines drawn there by sleepless nights spent beside his hospital bed.

Ten months after their first visit to see the doctor the family said their final earthly "good-byes" to Randy. They left the hospital room with an ache in their hearts and a vacancy at the breakfast table.

But they did not walk alone. Randy's triumphant faith would accompany them the rest of their lives.

Ten months is a long time in the life of a young person, too long to spend dying. Randy spent it living. He faced the future unafraid. His was not a surface bravado, but the result of a deep, personal commitment to Jesus Christ. Of course, there were times of great discouragement, for Randy wanted to live and be a normal person. Not long before his death he heard his father say to his mother, "Honey, he is going to be with the Lord." The boy roused from his coma and said, "But I want to stay with you guys." Yet, even in the depth of depression, there was light in his eye and peace in his heart. His honest Christian faith attracted the attention and admiration of the entire hospital staff. When Randy died, they suddenly realized they had lost more than a patient. They had lost a resevoir of hope and optimism.

In his short life, Randy demonstrated the truth of the words of the apostle Paul, who said, "Our earthly bodies, the ones we have now that can die, must be transformed into heavenly bodies that cannot perish but will live forever. When this happens . . . death is swallowed up in victory" (1 Cor. 15:53-54, TLB).

The prayer chapel built in Randy's memory is now complete. It stands in an honored spot just north of the sanctuary where he sang with the teen choir. It will be a lasting tribute to his faith.

But there is a greater tribute. It was given to him by a

crusty cancer specialist who disguised his emotions with his profanity. He had been with Randy from the beginning, and was there at the end. He had seen it all, the joy and the sorrow, the good days and the bad. But most of all, he had seen a young man who loved Jesus Christ more than life itself.

When it was all over, someone asked the doctor, "What did you learn from Randy's case?"

He replied, "We didn't learn very much about leukemia, but we learned an awful lot about how to live!"

Death gives meaning to life. It gives it dimension, dignity, and the dynamic of a new power; a power available through the resurrection of our Lord and Savior Jesus Christ.

6/

The End of the Road
— and Beyond

Sitting in the air-conditioned splendor of a Dallas hotel room, Sitka, Alaska, seemed far away and friendly. But it did not seem that way to a young couple who had followed God's call to that remote town.

At least, not at first.

Sitka is on an island off the coast of Alaska, with Juneau and Ketchikan as its closest neighbors across the inland strait. Fishing, timber, and tourists are the major industries, the order of importance depending on the time of year. During the summer, the ferry carrying hundreds of vehicles stops in the harbor nearly every day. It is an exciting place to live. Unexpectedly, and quite often, a tourist will call from downtown to bring news from Duluth, Detroit, or Dallas.

And downtown is not far away. There are only 14 miles

of road on the entire island. Summer is a time of happy surprises for those who live on this northern outpost.

Back in Dallas, the young couple relaxed in the hotel room with some of their closest friends. Even now, having been "outside" for about a month, Sitka seemed far away.

Friendly? Well, that was another story. Tomorrow they would return, back to the island, the place of isolation. For, while summer brings tourists, winter brings loneliness.

Contemplating their return, they suddenly became very quiet. The sound from the television program the children were watching engulfed them, filling the awkward silence.

The wife struggled to explain, unsuccessfully fighting back her tears. She talked about the isolation, the loneliness, the emotional depression they experienced when the flow of visitors ceased. From then until spring, expect for an occasional ship, the only way to the mainland was by air, and their budget could not finance many trips.

As fall comes to Sitka, the weather grows cold, and gray, and wet. Day after day it rains, and with it comes an oppresive feeling of gloom.

Without warning the couple's nine-year-old boy became critically ill with an unknown virus during a Sitka autumn. The doctors were confused and advised that Peter be flown out to Seattle. But the weather wouldn't allow the flight. It would be days before their boy could be taken to a better-equipped hospital.

Then the phone went dead. The doctors were unable to contact specialists in Seattle for advice. The distraught parents spent the most agonizing 48 hours of their life until their son's condition suddenly and miraculously improved.

A few days later they took Peter home from the small hospital. A carefully supervised recovery period brought him back to full health. But the fear remained, the terrible lonely feeling of being totally cut off from everything that spoke to them of peace and security.

Looking down at central Dallas from their 15th-floor hotel room the wife and mother said, "It was months before we drove to the end of the road." Only 14 miles of road on the island and they were reluctant to drive the last mile. The end of the road was the final, grim reminder of their remote prison.

Months went by. Hardly a dish was washed that was not baptized by her hot, sad tears. The lonely days were matched by sleepless nights. In the process things changed. Their friends at the church were aware of their emotional struggle. Many of them had also gone through a tough period of transition. They gave them their love and understanding. Gradually, fear melted away until one December day they drove to the end of the road with a keen sense of anticipation and returned with a glow of happiness. Because of the loving support of someone who understood, who had been there, they had been able to conquer their fear. Now they drive there often, unload their trail-bike and explore the wilderness beyond.

They were not the first to conquer their fear of the unknown. Many nations have been carved out of the wilderness. Some nations mark their beginning by the historical accident of geographical nearness. The United States of America is a classic example. Once the door had been opened by the fortune hunters of Europe, a steady stream of land-hungry families sailed through it to the new world.

The new settlers were a diverse lot. Some came to find freedom of worship, only to deny it to anyone who differed from them. Others came to find freedom from English jails or French justice. The poor came with little to lose but their future. The rich came looking for new markets or a shortcut to wealth. From all over western Europe they came, seeking a new beginning in a big, empty land.

Early America may have been the "land of opportunity," but it soon became clear that it took more than a trip across the Atlantic to change the nature of a man. They were prompted by the same jealousies, motivated by the same hatreds, and hobbled by the same fears they had known in the land of their birth. Soon there were 13 small, struggling colonies competing against each other more than against any distant monarch. Huddled together on a narrow strip of land between the Atlantic Ocean and the Allegheny Mountains, they were not a nation and had no plans to become one.

They were, however, neighbors. By an historical accident, they had been thrown together, a few lonely people on the edge of a mystery. Gradually they began to cooperate, out of necessity, not brotherhood. Eventually they would fight together for their freedom, and much later they would fight each other to define the limits of that freedom. Even at the beginning, they did not fight for a common cause. They battled the British in the spirit of a phrase made famous more than 150 years later by a man who became president of the republic. Dwight David Eisenhower said that the United States should act out of "enlightened self-interest." They did not know the motto, but they marched together, held tightly by the cohesive force of that human dynamic.

The United States became a nation by the historical accident of geographical nearness. But it was different for the Hebrews. They became a nation on the strength of a divine promise.

It began with a dream, a vision that sought to be reborn. Once it had existed, if only for a little while, in the mind of a man named Terah. It was strong enough to lead him out of Ur of Chaldees toward a better future. That promise evaporated in a small patch of green surrounded by the parched desert when his son Haran died. He stopped to mourn his loss and never again had the courage to pursue the challenge that had called him that far.

When Terah died that dream was bequeathed to his son

51

Abram. Not by man, but by God. When the proper ceremonies for the dead had been completed and Abram was at the point of decision, the angel came to him with a great promise. The descendants of that lonely man have either lived under the weight or have been guided by the light of that promise, since the fateful moment when Abram chose to go west to the future.

Some nations mark their beginning by the historical accident of geographical nearness, but not the Hebrews. They were "marching to Canaan, beautiful, beautiful Canaan."

But that was a long time ago. By the time of Jesus they knew the unbearable sadness of a faded dream. No longer did they live in a "land of promise." Their homeland had become the training ground for the armies of the world. It had often been destroyed, their beloved Temple defiled. The exciting dreams they had for their nation lay crushed under a Roman heel. They held in their hands the cold ashes of an empty hope. Their inheritance was a shambles.

Our generation also knows what it means for a dream to go sour. William Brownson has captured the mood of the age in these starkly honest words, "We have seen what happened at Dachau and Auschwitz, at Pearl Harbor and Hiroshima. We've watched with horror at the arms race and the arming of the races. Our dreams have been smashed and a dark cynicism has stolen upon us. The hope that flourished in the optimism of the nineteenth century lies dead."[1]

Behind a haughty exterior, our frightened world has gone looking for hope. They have wrung the last ounce from every illicit passion, ingested every illegal drug, and rallied around every promised savior. Once emotion surged across our college campuses and ran wild in the streets. They saw hope for the future in every burned-out hulk, in the destruction of anything that connected today with yesterday.

Now the demonstrations have ceased and the demonstrators have retired. A dreary silence has fallen on the lives of a great host of people. The epidemic use of beverage alcohol that has swept the country is but a feeble attempt to numb the spirit and mask the hopelessness that has invaded the world.

"But not all hopes die," William Brownson has happily observed.

An elderly woman was face-to-face with her last hours. To her husband of more than 50 years she said, "John, come with me, won't you?"

With eyes filled with tears, he replied, "Anna, I cannot go. Only Jesus can go with you."

The words of the loving husband are words of sadness, but they are not the weak words of a quitter. They are the strong words of faith. In fact, the Christian faith has no stronger words than those written by Peter, who announced to a group of depressed and persecuted Christians that there was a "living hope" in Christ. He wrote, "Praise be to the God and Father of our Lord Jesus Christ! In his great mercy he has given us new birth into a living hope through the resurrection of Jesus Christ from the dead, and into an inheritance that can never perish, spoil, or fade— kept in heaven for you" (1 Pet. 1:3-4, NIV).

The old law with its complicated ritual and continual animal sacrifice required constant death to have any degree of freedom from death and the smallest spark of hope. The new "law" in Christ offers life as the same source of freedom from guilt and hope as bright as the promises of God— here and hereafter.

When the believers in Corinth began to doubt the reality and the significance of Christ's resurrection, Paul declared, "If Christ was not raised, then our gospel is null and void, and so is your faith . . . if Christ was not raised, your faith has nothing in it and you are still in your old state of sin. It follows also that those who have died within Christ's fellowship are utterly lost. If it is for this life only that Christ has given us hope, we of all men are most to be pitied" (1 Cor. 15:13-14, 16-19, NEB).

For the apostle, the Resurrection was the most significant Y in life's road. Ultimate destiny depended on which fork of the road you followed. To the Corinthians, and many today, the choice does not appear to be crucial. As in many other decisions of life, though, its importance is not understood completely until you come to the end of the road.

Several pastors were on their way to go deer hunting early one Monday morning. It was still dark when they turned off the highway east of Redding, Calif., for Bosworth Meadows. Since none of them had been in that country before, they were following directions hastily scratched on the back of an envelope.

At first the road was easy to follow. The landmarks were identifiable; a house here, a dead tree there, a bridge. They made rapid progress. But when they had driven far enough into the mountains to leave all the evidence of civilization behind them, the decisions became more difficult.

Unexpectedly, the driver stopped. In front of them was a fork in the road. Which way? No one knew. A happy, but lively argument followed. Finally they took a vote and the driver turned in the direction indicated by the majority.

The countryside looked the same, and since none of them had been there before they could not refer to any landmarks for guidance. They only knew that Bosworth Meadows was to be at the end of the road.

But not at the end of that road. It disappeared into a rubble of dirt, rock, and charred brush. In the dim light of early dawn the preachers saw the bare ground and blackened hillside where a fire had devasted the area.

They found Bosworth Meadows, but only after they retraced that rutted dirt road to the Y and turned the proper way.

Life is like that. Sometimes you do not know the importance of the fork in the road until you get to the end. When a person decides that the resurrection of Christ is only of marginal importance, then, Paul says, the gospel is null and void, the dead are forever lost, our faith is useless, there is no hope and we have only pity for comfort. That is small consolation when faced with a mountain of grief.

But if we believe that "Christ died for our sins, in accordance with the scriptures; that he was buried; that he was raised to life on the third day" (1 Cor. 15:3-4, NEB), then, as Peter proclaimed, we have been given new birth, a living hope, and inheritance in heaven which cannot be destroyed, will not spoil nor wither.

The resurrection of Christ makes the difference. His resurrection transforms tomorrow. In ancient Greece, before the coming of Christianity, the dead were buried with their faces toward the setting sun. But with the promise of the Christian faith, the believers began to bury their friends and loved ones with their faces toward the rising sun. Hope!

In an exciting way, the reality of the Resurrection gives us a tomorrow toward which we can walk unafraid. Thus, at Easter we respond with joy to the choir's triumphant refrain, "Because He lives, I can face tomorrow."

The resurrection of Jesus Christ is not just another isolated happening in the varied life of the Galilean. To be sure, every incident in His life is important to give a well-rounded picture. Christ at the marriage at Cana, or talking with the many-times-married matron of Samaria reveals His "human" side. Knowing this aspect of His personality, it is easier to believe that Jesus can understand us, that He cares. There is nothing we know about the Master that is unimportant.

Yet not all of the information that the Bible contains about Jesus is of equal value. He would still be our Savior if we knew nothing about the wedding at Cana or the conversation by Jacob's Well. But erase the Resurrection from the pages of time, and He is no longer Lord and Master. He is only a minor revolutionary in a remote, second-class Roman province.

Jesus had to die before He could be the resurrected Savior. The Resurrection is painted in warm, happy colors; sung to the melodic strains of the harp. However, on Calvary there was the crash of anger and the blackness of burned-out dreams. It is worth noting that our hope for the future is rooted as much in the angry black of Calvary as in the joyful gold of the empty tomb. For anyone who faces the anxiety and fear of an uncertain future, Christ can bring comfort; He has been there, too. Seen in perspective, there is as much comfort in Calvary as in the Resurrection for all who face the tough reality of imminent death. That was an important truth a man and his pastor learned in a most dramatic way.

The man lay dying with abdominal cancer. The months had dragged by, draining him of the strength of his middle years. He was frail, gray, emaciated—a hollow form filled with fear and bitterness. His wife had been unable to face his physical disintegration and had sought comfort in the arms of another man.

Two days before he died he said to his pastor, "I am afraid to die. I don't know whether God will let me into heaven or not."

The pastor replied, rather lamely, "Well, everyone has their fears."

As that pastor drove back to his study he became increasingly disatisfied with his advice to his dying friend. He tried to change the focus of his thinking as he arrived at his office, for he had only a few hours to prepare to speak at the community Good Friday service. But he could not concentrate. The emptiness of his answer kept intruding into his thoughts.

In that mood, and under that cloud, he read the words of Jesus on the cross, "My God, my God, why hast thou forsaken me?" (Matt. 24:46).

Suddenly he could not see Jesus on the cross. He could see only a frightened man who lay on a white sheet, barely kept alive through the hardware and plumbing of modern medicine.

Then it hit him like a boxer's blow to the pit of the stomach. The cry of Christ on the cross was just like the cry he had heard in the hospital. Here was Christ at His point of greatest humanity, His supreme identification with men. For the first time the pastor understood the words of Hebrews, He "has been tempted in every way, just as we are" (Heb. 4:15, NIV).

Christ frightened? Afraid of the future? The minister had heard the words of Christ from the lips of his parishioner when he said, "Pastor, I'm afraid to die, I don't know whether God will let me into His heaven or not."

His study was filled with despair, the terrible black despair that smothered Calvary and snuffed out the world's light for three hours on that fateful Friday.

Then, just as suddenly, the darkness melted away as he recalled that shortly after that cry of dereliction Christ said to His father, "Into your hands I commit my spirit" (Luke 23:46, NIV). Christ had driven to the end of the road and was willing to trust the "beyond" to the Father.

Quickly the pastor ran to his car and rushed back to the hospital. Now he had something to say. Now the frightened man could die in peace. Christ was with him on that bed. He knew what he was experiencing. Jesus had been there, faced the fear and the future. He had gone to the end of the road.

That is why we Christians rejoice. Our faith is not in a proposition but in a person. That Person announced one night, "Let not your heart be troubled: ye believe in God, believe also in me. . . . I go to prepare a place for you" (John

14:1-2). It is as if Jesus said, "I will go to the end of the road —and beyond; and because I go there in strength, you can go there in your weakness." Thus the apostle Paul wrote, "I want to know Christ and the power of his resurrection and the fellowship of sharing in his sufferings, becoming like him in his death, and so, somehow, to attain to the resurrection from the dead" (Phil. 3:10-11, NIV).

It is clear that for Paul and his Christian contemporaries the Resurrection was not simply an event to be accepted, a doctrine to be believed. It was a resevoir of power for daily living.

Yet Paul did not claim to understand it completely, for he wrote to the Corinthains, "Now we see through a glass darkly" (1 Cor. 13:12). Indeed, this is a magnificent mystery, the inevitable, glorious conclusion of our Christian faith.

7/

The Magnificent Mystery

There were many things little Hansi did not know, for she was only in the second grade. The words, "Heil Hitler!" had no meaning to her, then, but would dominate her life much later when she gladly followed the swastika. Nor could she imagine the peace and joy belief in Christ would bring one day, for that was so far in the future.

As a child, Hansi's world consisted primarily of a foster mother she loved, a foster father she feared, and a foster brother who appeared to hate her.

She was a nobody, an orphan. Her mother dead, deserted by her father, she was an extra mouth to feed in a home that was already living at the level of near starvation. The harried foster father, unable to adequately feed his own family, made no attempt to hide his hostility toward Hansi.

The only love she knew came from her compassionate foster mother, a devout Christian.

Hansi learned to pray in that troubled home. Alone in her bed in the hayloft, she would try to enlist God's help, asking only for the most basic things in life. Always she finished her simple prayer by asking the Lord to "send my guardian angel by my bed, Amen."

Then, she recalls, "When I opened my eyes I tried again my favorite, but always unsuccessful, trick. Mother, who had taught me how to pray, had also told me that God and the angels could not be seen. But I was certain they must become visible whenever I closed my eyes. So I always tried to open my eyes very slowly or so quickly after prayer that I might catch a glimpse of the heavenly visitor before they disappeared again. I was never fast enough to catch even the last shimmer of an angel wing."[1]

To catch an angel's wing is the desire of every man, and has been since the dawn of time. In their own way and against the background of their culture, every man has tried to decipher the mystery of the universe—to catch an angel's wing. Man has both feared and worshipped the unknown. Primitive societies defied the forces of nature, giving costly gifts to appease the gods. In some cultures, these consisted of the ultimate sacrifice, a human life.

The Aztecs, early residents of Mexico, had an unending variety of religious ceremonies where humans were sacrificed. The victim, usually either a prisoner of war or a slave, was stretched over a sacrificial stone and his heart removed. Small children, five or six years of age, were thought to be preferred by the rain gods. Prior to sacrifice, they were dressed in the best jewels and finest clothes the community could afford.

The Aztecs believed that the sun god lost its flesh each night. They thought it necessary to sacrifice humans so that their flesh and blood would reclothe the bones of the skeleton sun as it emerged from the underworld of darkness.

Their religious beliefs forced them to fight many wars in order to maintain the supply of prisoners to sacrifice. This practice reached unbelievable extremes. At the dedication of the great pyramid and temple of Tenochtitlan, 20,000 prisoners were sacrificed.

The same fear of the unknown motivated the Aztec priest to hold a still-beating heart heavenward; an early North American to send a beautiful young maiden over Niagara Falls; and a member of an occult society in the Carribbean to kidnap a young blond child to use in satisfying the anger of the gods.

Black magic is, even now, a powerful force in many of the emerging nations of Africa. A few years ago, when a whale beached itself on the African coast near Accra, the president of Ghana, Kwame Nkrumah, and his cabinent attended the funeral. The fishermen of Ghana believe that the whale is a lesser god of the sea which, if properly honored, will fill their nets with fish. Thus, for both political and religious reasons, a dead whale had a royal escort at its burial.

Strange. Perhaps. But not to people who fear the unknown and worship the mysterious. It is so real that people still stick pins in dolls, dance feverishly to the beat of the drum until they drop from exhaustion, and pay the voodoo priest a year's wages to ward off evil.

Unusual customs have resulted. The Aguaruna Indians of Peru believe that if you want to live to an old age you should eat one-half of a turtle's heart; if you want to be physically strong you grind up the bones of an anteater and add them to your diet.

Soldiers have gone into battle confident that they would not die because the priest had sprinkled "holy water" on them, and some fishermen are convinced that an annual religious ritual on the wharf guarantees a good season.

Both of these customs are a part of the sophisticated culture of the 20th century, not some primitive society in a remote tropical rain forest.

To catch an angel's wing has consumed a significant portion of the wealth and energy of every society. Everyone, in every age and generation, has had their own method of coping with the mystery of life.

The Bible does not deny the mystery. The Old Testament has many examples of a bewildered nation seeking guidance. There is Moses on the top of Mount Sinai, and King Saul seeking advice from the witch of Endor; Joseph interpreting the meaning of the king's dreams, and Daniel translating the words written on Belshazzar's banquet wall; Abraham standing on the mountain about to plunge a knife into the heart of his son, and Job sitting on an ash heap scraping at his boils with a shard of pottery—all trying to decipher a baffling universe.

The Bible does not deny the mystery, nor does it apologize for it. It recognizes it as a part of the human situation. In fact, Paul wrote to the Corinthians, "Now we see through a glass darkly" (1 Cor. 13:12).

Anyone can ask questions that cannot be answered—that even God cannot answer. The scholastics of the Dark Ages argued over such questions: "Can God build a rock so heavy that He cannot lift it?" or, "How many angels can sit on the head of a pin?"

There are modern questions that, likewise, cannot be answered. "How many bushels are there in a mile?" "What is the square root of a quart of milk?" So many of our questions are like that. Not even God can answer them, for they are nonsense questions. They do not challenge the ability of the one who is queried, but reveal the limited knowledge of the questioner.

Some of the questions we ask each other in our sorrow, and sometimes in our anger, are likewise unanswerable, for the answer has its feet in a dramatically different kind of existence. "Now we see through a glass, darkly; but then face to face: now I know in part; but then shall I know even as also I am known" (1 Cor. 13:12).

Fanny Crosby, the gifted songwriter, caught the beauty of this promise in these glad words,

> Someday the silver cord will break,
> And I no more as now shall sing.
> But, oh, the joy when I shall wake
> Within the palace of the King!

And the refrain comes lilting back,

> And I shall see Him face-to-face,
> And tell the story—Saved by grace.

The apostle said it a long time ago, "Eye hath not seen, nor ear heard, neither have entered into the heart of man, the things which God hath prepared for them that love him" (1 Cor. 2:9).

The fact that the mystery exists is encouraging. It is a magnificent mystery. It shouts to all who listen that this universe is not limited to the dimensions of a man's mind.

Give him credit, mankind has pushed back the borders of ignorance much farther than anyone dreamed possible. His achievements have been outstanding. Yet he has not reduced the size of the mystery. Every advance in knowledge has revealed a new "unknown." Significantly, that "unknown" has been a part of God's universe from the beginning and men have just learned enough to discover the existence of something else they did not understand.

Out of the mystery, God came in the person of His Son, Jesus. He brought the mystery with Him. To one of the most knowledgeable scholars of His time Jesus said, "You should not be surprised at my saying, 'You must be born again.' The wind blows wherever it pleases. You may hear its sound, but you cannot tell where it comes from or where it is going" (John 3:7-8, NIV).

In his invigorating sermon "The Wind of the Spirit," James Stewart says,

> Some want to eliminate the element of mystery and the dimension of transcendence. They would prefer to have the Father-in-heaven image replaced by a statement about human self-awareness. . . . So we rationalise and psychologise and demythologise—until the Christian faith has ceased to be the good news about a living personal God acting in history and has become merely something about man and his nature, and his so-called authentic existence; until theology is lost itself in anthropology; until perhaps we reach the point of the self-confident journalist who wrote, 'We now know there is no such thing as the supernatural.' How astonishingly naive! How frightfully callow! As if there were nothing in the world than our logic could measure or our intelligence could explore! As if man's self-awareness were the soul and center of the universe! Jesus here says to us, as He said to Nicodemus—stop explaining, and worship! Stop arguing and adore.[2]

Religion, especially the religion of Jesus Christ, does not clear up our mysteries. It was never intended to do that. On the contrary, the deepest mystery of it all is the Cross, the mystery that issues out of the crash of anger on a blood-spattered hill where three crosses were jammed into their stone sockets in hate. That mystery brings life and light. Light enough to walk by, light enough for the next step.

A Vermont man tells of the experience of his younger days. On his own for the first time, he had taken a job in a distant city where he had neither friends nor relatives. During the day he was too busy to think of home. But sometimes at night he would become overwhelmed with his loneliness. Like a magnet he would be drawn to the railroad station. Standing on the platform looking at the rails in the direction of home he would begin to feel better. He knew that if he followed those rails far enough, he would be reunited with those he loved.[3]

Lloyd Douglas has caught the mood of modern man when, in *The Robe*, he has the Roman soldier Marcellus say to his slave, "I am inclined to agree with you, Demetrius. It would be a great comfort, though if—especially in an hour of bewilderment—one could nourish a reasonable hope that a benevolent Power existed—somewhere—and might be invoked."[4]

Christians believe that they have found that hope. As Paul expressed it, "The time of my death has come. I have fought the good fight; I have finished the race; I have kept the faith. Beyond that there is laid away for me the crown of righteousness which the Lord, the righteous judge, will award me in that Day, and not to me alone, but to all who have loved His appearing" (2 Tim. 4:6-8, NBV).

Bret Harte confesses that he was afraid of death until he caught the vision of it in the words of Paul. Encouraged by Paul's faith at the time of his departure, the poet wrote concerning his own,

> *I hear from the outgoing ships in the bay*
> *The song of the sailors in glee:*
> *And wait for the signal to go to the shore*
> *To the ship that is waiting for me.*[5]

The Bible does not deny the mystery, nor does it apologize for it. It recognizes it as a part of the human situation, a mystery that is happily drained of its fear. The One who was hated enough to be killed—soon to be betrayed, whipped, and crucified—said in the final hours He had with His closest friends, "These things have I spoken unto you, that my joy might remain in you, and that your joy might be full" (John 15:11).

When the final mystery was closing in on Christ, He talked about joy. He could face the ultimate challenge, knowing that He was not alone. In that confidence, He gave assurance to the disciples. Earlier He had said, "I am the door"; now He affirms, "I am the way, the truth, and the life" (John 14:6). Thus, with confidence He encouraged them, "Let not your heart be troubled . . . I go to prepare a place for you. And if I go and prepare a place for you, I will come again, and receive you unto myself; that where I am, there ye may be also" (John 14:2-3).

His promise was an open door to future happiness; His heritage, peace. "Peace I leave with you, my peace I give unto you: not as the world giveth, give I unto you. Let not your heart be troubled, neither let it be afraid" (John 14:27).

The means of achieving that "Promised Land" is one of the paradoxes of the Christian faith. One of the greatest. "The hour is come," Christ announced, "that the Son of man should be glorified." Then He added, "Except a corn of wheat fall into the ground and die, it abideth alone: but if it die, it bringeth forth much fruit" (John 12:23-24). We may not understand all that this teaching means, but we are encouraged by the continuation of the individual beyond the grave and the opportunities for personal growth. Paul responded to that golden chord with this glad refrain, "We are looking all the time not at the visible things but at the invisible. The visible things are transitory: it is the invisible things that are really permanent. We know, for instance, that if our earthly dwelling were taken down, like a tent, we have a permanent house in Heaven, made, not by man, but by God" (2 Cor. 4:18—5:1, Phillips).

Death is the impenetrable mystery. But it is not omnipotent. It is not the most powerful force in the universe. We are encouraged by these words: "I am convinced that neither death nor life . . . nor anything else in all creation, will be able to seperate us from the love of God that is in Christ Jesus our Lord" (Rom. 8:38-39, NIV).

This is reminiscent of the lady in a wheelchair who was

asked, "Is this a permanent disability, are you going to be in that wheelchair all your life?"

She replied with a smile, "No, just till I get to heaven."

God uses different punctuation marks than we do. An example came early in Hebrew history. "Now after the death of Moses the servant of the Lord it came to pass, that the Lord spake unto Joshua the son of Nun, Moses' minister, saying, Moses my servant is dead; now therefore arise, go over this Jordan" (Josh. 1:1-2).

Where they had put a period, God inserted a comma. It was not over, there was just a temporary pause. There are so many good things God wants to give His people, when they desire His will, when they "set [their] affection on things above, not on things on the earth" (Col. 3:2).

The life that God wants to give His children, and the way it is obtained, is illustrated by a trip a man took to see his 80-year-old grandmother. As an amateur collector of old things, he admired an unusual oak table which graced her living room. He said, "Someday I'd like to have that table."

She replied, "Please take it now."

He declined, indicating that if he should outlive her, he would like to receive it. She insisted that he take it immediately, so she would know he had received it.

As he tried to express his appreciation she stopped him, saying quietly, "Thank you for wanting it."

To all who accept His promise of life, Jesus says, "Thank you for wanting it."

Truly it is a magnificent mystery. Our religion does not clear up the mystery, nor does it give us a formula that will answer all our questions. But "in the meantime there is light enough to live by."[6] And that is good; for ours is a disposable society.

8/

Our Disposable Society

Seven carefully packed boxes sat casually on a neighbor's front porch. The owner would need their contents no longer. She had been buried the previous day.

The boxes contained the entire wardrobe of a retired physical education teacher. Her clothes were practical, but not inexpensive, and they showed that during her 63 years she had developed an appreciation for quality.

It was evident to anyone who stopped to notice that a loving sister had packed them with care. There was a special kind of dignity even at this faceless moment of transition.

NOTE: This chapter appeared first in *High*, Mar. 23, 1975. Used here by permission of Harvest Publications, Evanston, Ill. Randy's story was added to the original article that appeared under the title "A Pile of Clothes, A Dried-up Lawn, A Moving Van," by Gene Van Note.

But most people did not pause to look inside the boxes. They saw only a cluttered assortment of cardboard cartons containing "somebody's old clothes."

Somebody's old clothes, indeed!

They were not "somebody's old clothes." They were *her* clothes. She had a name and a face. She was a person of value, a neighbor and a friend. She was not a "discard" to be recycled to a lower economic level.

The evidence, however, seemed to dispute that statement. She had selected her wardrobe carefully. It was extension of her personality, reflecting her income and life-style. But now those individually-selected items sat in a pile on a porch waiting for a disinterested third party to transport them to a private welfare agency. There they would be dumped out on a table and sorted according to size and quality.

And when it happened, the first comment was, "Boy, she must have smoked a lot." It was true. She was a chain-smoker, and that might have been a factor in the cancer which drained life from her at an early age. Yet her 63 years of skill in selecting proper clothes was dismissed by an off-hand comment about her smoking habit.

So they gave away her clothes and put a "For Sale" sign on the front lawn they neglected to water. She would have understood the sign, for she was unmarried. But the lawn had been her joy and pride, the source of community approval since it was the most attractive yard in the neighborhood. Now it was turning brown from a lack attention.

A pile of clothes, a dried-up lawn, a moving van containing her furniture to be divided among the family or sold at a garage sale, and she ceased to be. All that remained was a memory in the heart of the people who loved her, the 20 who had attended the funeral and perhaps a few more.

A pile of clothes, a dried-up lawn, and a moving van. Is

this what life is all about? Selected portions of the Bible would seem to support that idea. James said, "The length of your lives is as uncertain as the morning fog" (Js. 4:14, TLB). The psalmist agreed when he wrote, "Man is no more than a puff of wind, his days as a passing shadow" (Ps. 144:4, NEB).

The contemporaries of Jesus seemed to confirm this when the high priest dismissed Him and His influence by saying, "it is better for you that one man die . . . than the whole nation perish" (John 11:50, NIV). Discard Him and He would cease to be.

A pile of clothes, a dried-up lawn, and a moving van; the idea has been around for a long time. Man is disposable. Perhaps no generation understands the implication of this more clearly than our disposable society. Manufactured items are not built to last; they are designed to deteriorate. Even under the pressure of the ecologists, "recycling" is more a dream than a reality. Like the words on the brown paper bag, man, too, is biodegradable!

The decision concerning Jesus was so simple. Every man is disposable; this one is also dispensable. Destroy Him, and His revolutionary ideas would disappear.

So they killed Him. But it did not work! The device designed to destroy Him became the measure of His victory. This man was neither dispensable nor disposable, and that shook history to the core.

But there was more, much more than even this radical event. Jesus said, "I am the resurrection and the life. He who believes in me will live, even though he dies; and whoever lives and believes in me will never die" (John 11:25-26, NIV). The implication of these words is tremendous. Man is not disposable. He is infinitely more than a pile of clothes, a dried-up lawn, and a moving van.

Jesus meant, among other things, that though life may be short, it is not little. A flash of lightning or the flash of a smile are both short, but neither is small. Both have altered history though their lifetime is measured in split seconds. Life is longer than either of them; but viewed against eternity, it is, as the Bible declares, "a puff of wind, a passing shadow, the morning fog."

Life is short, but it is not little. A modern sage has observed, "Life is too short to be little." Man was made for bigger things. He is not a disposable item. Since Jesus intercepted history, life must be measured by some standard other than length. His own victory over death provides both the inspiration and the possibility for all who believe in Him to find their own personal victory.

Do you remember Randy? You met him in chapter five. It has been three years now since he said to his mother, "He hasn't come, but I'm ready."

"Who hasn't come, and what are you waiting for?" his mother asked and was comforted then, and now, to hear her dying son reply, "The Lord; I'm waiting for the Lord."

And soon the Lord came.

Now, three years later, Randy's father remembers those "terrible last weeks when we faced the reality of death itself. It *was* terrible." Then he adds, wistfully, "I wouldn't wish him back for anything when I think with my mind, but with my heart I long to see him come through the door."

At the time of bereavement, and following, it is the heart and not the mind that speaks most loudly. C. S. Lewis observed, "You tell me that 'she goes on.' But my heart and body are crying out, come back, come back." He continues, "No one ever told me that grief felt so like fear. I am not afraid, but the sensation is like being afraid. The same fluttering in the stomach, the same restlessness, the yawning. I keep on swallowing. There is an invisible blanket between the world and me."[1]

Time passes. Friends give their love. The Bible takes on

new meaning. The Lord is near. The promises of the Word are proved true.

"Come unto me, all ye that labour and are heavy laden, and I will give you rest" (Mat. 11:28). Time does not do all the healing. The Lord does not disappoint. In Him there is hope. As missionary Maurice Hall commented about leaving his black friends after 19 years in Africa, "Christians never say 'good-bye' for the last time."

It is the strength of this faith, its working reality, that has enabled Randy's father to write, "There are so many things that have happened as a result of his illness that it is all like one great big master design. We still miss him very much, but there *is* special comfort to the person in Christ. It doesn't keep us from being human, but there is a dimension that gives meaning to life."

Wallace was just a 16-year-old farm boy on the top of a load of hay. Two older brothers and his father were down below forking the hay up to him to stack. It was like any other late summer day on the farm in central Michigan in the early years of this century.

Not many days earlier Wallace had knelt at the "mourner's bench" at a local camp meeting. He had come to pray, to clear accounts with his Maker. His faith had found perfect root that day.

Without warning a small thunderstorm burst around them in the field. The three on the ground raced across the stubble to the safety of the barn while Wallace urged the horses down the lane.

The brutal tragedy of the blinding flash of lightning was known soon enough as the horses came violently into the barnyard with a load of smoking hay, but no driver.

Soon the entire family had gathered around the lifeless figure of a 16-year-old boy. What happened next cannot be understood by a skeptical world. They bowed their heads and praised God. They had their private camp meeting.

Strange behavior in the presence of death?

Yes, and no.

Were they happy that Wallace was dead? No, of course not. They were praising God that their loved one had found a faith by which to die. Such a faith does not thumb its nose at death as if to deny its reality, nor does it lift its hat as one would welcome a friend. Such a faith faces the future with confidence, knowing that death, for the Christian, is not a pile of clothes, a dried-up lawn, and a moving van. Death is the end, but it is·more. It is the glorious beginning of the believer's new life in Christ, a richer life beyong this world of sin and sorrow in the presence of the Savior himself.

Reference Notes

CHAPTER 2:

1. Charles L. Wallis, ed., *The Funeral Encyclopedia* (New York: Harper and Bros., 1953), p. 126.

2. Paul S. Rees, *Things Unshakable* (Grand Rapids: Wm. B. Eerdmans Pub. Co., 1947), p. 148.

3. C. S. Lewis, *A Grief Observed* (New York: The Seabury Press, 1961), p. 15.

4. "Let's Talk About Death," pamphlet prepared by the Christophers, 12 E. 48th St., New York, N.Y.

5. Howard L. Stimmel, *Rendezvous with Eternity* (New York: Abingdon-Cokesbury Press, 1947), p. 62.

6. Lewis, *Grief Observed*, p. 19.

7. *Ibid*, p. 60.

8. Janet Kern, "When You Write Letters of Condolence," *Guideposts*, Mar., 1960.

CHAPTER 3:

1. William Barclay, *The Daily Study Bible*, "The Letter to the Hebrews" (Philadelphia: The Westminster Press, 1957), p. 16.

2. Harry Emerson Fosdick, *Riverside Sermons* (New York: Harper and Bros., 1958), p. 156.

3. J. Wallace Hamilton, *Serendipity* (Westwood, N.J.: Fleming H. Revell Co., 1965), p. 35.

4. W. T. Purkiser, *When You Get to the End of Yourself* (Kansas City: Beacon Hill Press of Kansas City, 1970), p. 22.

CHAPTER 4:

1. Lloyd C. Douglas, *The Robe* (Boston: Houghton Mifflin Co., 1947), p. 135.

2. "Creativity, Fear of Death Linked, Psychologists Say," article by Eleanor Hoover in the *Los Angeles Times*, Sept. 8, 1975.

3. William Barclay, *In the Hands of God* (New York: Harper and Row, Pub., 1967), pp. 106-7.

4. Felix Marti-Ibanez, "A Doctor Looks at Death." *Reader's Digest*, Mar., 1964.

CHAPTER 5:

1. Lloyd John Ogilvie, *Let God Love You* (Waco, Tex.: Word Books, 1974), p. 46.

2. Marti-Ibanez, "A Doctor Looks at Death."

3. William Evans, *Looking Beyond* (Chicago: Moody Press, 1932), p. 100.

4. Ogilvie, *God Loves You*, p. 46.

5. Aaron N. Mechel, *Living Can Be Exciting* (New York: E. P. Dutton and Co., Inc., 1956), p. 248.

CHAPTER 6:

1. William C. Brownson, *Tried by Fire* (Grand Rapids: Baker Book House, 1972), p. 34.

CHAPTER 7:

1. Adapted from Maria Anne Hirschmann, *Hansi, the Girl Who Loved the Swatiska* (Wheaton, Ill.: Tyndale House Publishers, 1973). Used by permission.

2. James S. Stewart, *The Wind of the Spirit* (Nashville: Abingdon Press, 1968), pp. 16-17.

3. Stimmel, *Rendezvous*, p. 30.

4. Douglas, *The Robe*, p. 39.

5. Evans, *Looking Beyond*, p. 97.

6. Fosdick, *Riverside Sermons*, p. 26.

CHAPTER 8:

1. Lewis, *Grief Observed*, p. 7.

Bibliography

Barclay, William. *The Daily Study Bible*, "The Letter to the Hebrews." Philadelphia: The Westminster Press, 1957.

———. *In the Hands of God*. New York: Harper and Row, Publishers, 1967.

Brownson, William C. *Tried by Fire*. Grand Rapids: Baker Book House, 1972.

Douglas, Lloyd. *The Robe*. Boston: Houghton Mifflin Co., 1947.

Evans, William. *Looking Beyond*. Chicago: Moody Press, 1932.

Hamilton, J. Wallace. *Serendipity*. Westwood, N.J.: Fleming H. Revell Co., 1965.

Hirschmann, Maria Anne. *Hansi, the Girl Who Loved the Swastika*. Wheaton, Ill.: Tyndale House Pub., 1974.

Hoover, Eleanor. "Creativity, Fear of Death Linked, Psychologists Say." *Los Angeles Times*, September 8, 1975.

Kern, Janet. "When You Write a Letter of Condolence." *Guideposts*, March, 1960.

Lewis, C. S. *A Grief Observed*. New York: The Seabury Press, 1961.

Marti-Ibanez, Felix. "A Doctor Looks at Death." *Reader's Digest*, March, 1964.

Meckel, Aaron N. *Living Can Be Exciting*. New York: E. P. Dutton and Co., Inc., 1956.

Ogilvie, Lloyd John. *Let God Love You*. Waco, Tex.: Word Books, 1974.

Purkiser, W. T. *When You Get to the End of Yourself*. Kansas City: Beacon Hill Press of Kansas City, 1970.

Rees, Paul S. *Things Unshakable*. Grand Rapids; Wm. B. Eerdmans Pub. Co., 1947.

Stewart, James S. *The Wind of the Spirit*. Nashville: Abingdon Press, 1968.

Stimmel, Howard L. *Rendezvous with Eternity*. New York: Abingdon-Cokesbury Press, 1947.